JN411217

Reflector

Sekyo Shim

My name is Sekyo Shim.

I was born in Korea in 2012, and I'm 13 years old.

When I was 6, my family moved to Toronto, Canada.

When I was in Toronto, I enrolled in Owen Public School.

I lived in Canada for 14 months before moving back to Korea.

Here in Korea, I graduated from Jeonju Onbit Elementary School

and now I'm a student in Jeonju Onbit Middle School.

Contents

Morning snow

I remember how it fell.
How it glistened in the light.
They never spoke but I could tell
that they'd been waiting all night.

Open the window.
I won't mind.
They never left a single shadow.
White is all I see on the ground.

It's clear white,
like diamond rays.
It's pure white,
like how angels pray.

It all came last year.
Will it ever come anytime later?
This time, I won't shiver.
No, not this winter.

I wave to you

I wave to you,
but you never do.
I speak to you,
but you never do.

Is it true that you hate me?
If so what have I done wrong,
or are you just one of the kids
who talk behind my back for fun?

Do you want to keep it cryptic?
Am I supposed to solve a riddle,
that's laced with your tactics
to keep me guessing in the middle?

Now it just feels awkward.
Seeing you in the hallway,
we're both walking forward.
You never look my way.

I wave to you,
but you never do.

The kingdom

The sun has risen once again.
I step into the enormous tower.
There isn't any authority for me to gain.
It's the dragons who have power.

It's fine; that's just how it flows,
in this little kingdom.
At certain times, the gate will close.
So, you see, nothing here's random.

Someday I'll get brave enough to be a knight.
Other days, I'll get scared and hide in the basement,
but the dragons in the garden never bite.
Unless you make the wrong movement.

Here, we take tests.
Sometimes it feels like ranking some bests.
It feels like testing our limits.
Unless you reach the summits.

However, something tells me this kingdom is worth
living in.
So, I guess there's a lot for me to win.

My arsenal

I've got all sorts of weapons.
Stilettos up my sleeves, slingshots in my pocket.
I can bring you to the war.
I've got a machine gun hidden up with a locket.

You think you have an army,
but what can you do with no armor?
Your blades aren't very charming.
So, bring it on, who's the first striker?

I'm now a master at avoiding cannonballs.
Your force can't destroy my city.
I'll catch you in my arsenal.
Let's not make this personal.

You don't even have a proper shield.
It'll take forever for you to heal.
I hope you realize this isn't a big deal,
so I won't ask you to kneel.

Neck high

"I'm fine. It's okay."
is the biggest lie I told today.
They can never understand.
I'm sailing and I don't see any land.

Would I not hurt if I never came back?
'Cause I don't want to see another part of me crack.
Real bad.
Maybe I'm mad.

To some I might be a girl who learns fast.
But to me, I'm just a girl who can't forget the past.
All the questions were mandatory,
and I can't make up ridiculous theories.

I feel like drowning in my old days.
Sometimes I can't see the sun rays.
Those days, I let out a long sigh,
'cause the water comes up neck high.

Best Protégé

I'm not the best protégé.
I'm a troublemaker someday.
Sometimes, my head won't work well,
but how can anyone ever tell
that my actions don't always obey?
And yet, I'm fine and okay
for the fact that
I'm not the best protégé.

I wasn't born to be the best protégé.
I was born to be myself.
I'm not for ringing the golden bell,
nor for having a legacy to tell.
Everyone knows it's my name,
and yet, I'm chill and okay
for the fact that
I'm not the best protégé.

Shiny, bright ’n pretty

I don’t need stupid invitations
to someone else’s house.
I don’t need my destination
to be someone else’s party.

I’ve got better things to spend my money on.
I don’t need trendy items other girls are on.
Why the ‘blending in’ fuss when that’s no fun.
I don’t need to entertain anyone else when I’m having fun.

To me, it’s boring, dull ’n plain.
Wouldn’t that be pain?
So, I love shiny, bright ’n pretty,
but that’s what you pity.

My aesthetics aren’t for the world.
They’re for no one other than me.
So, stifle in your sword,
’cause problems, I don’t see.

Dodge the bullet

"If you miss the ball,
you gotta dodge the bullet,"
everyone said in the hall,
but who are you to shoot the bullet?

You pull on the trigger
just to fill that empty hole,
but that only grows bigger
and I know that ain't your goal.

Your goal is to feel whole in the inside.
So you need someone to blame.
When so, you need friends on your side
to save yourself from shame.

Frantic

I see blinks of memory light.
I see them when I close my eyes.
Back then, I took my surroundings for granted,
but now, holding on to the flashbacks, I'm frantic.

Frantic, I'll lose them.
Frantic, I'll leave them.
I'm treasuring them like gems.
That's why it's mayhem.

Frantic, I'll lose my grip.
Frantic, I'll leave and trip.
I'm afraid the sheets might rip,
but I'm desperate.

Your aviation

Don't wanna see you down.
Remember your side when panting.
Your name is out loud,
that'll be us chanting.

Really, you're doing the world.
Not anyone can do it.
One day, we'll all dance and twirl.
By spotlights, you'll be lit.

A standing ovation.
Remember, you're not alone.
This is your aviation.
We'll fly with you as drones.

Really, you've got this.
We'll never stop cheering.
We'll be flashlights in the mist,
so, there's nothing you should be fearing.

Most prized possession

Does she know it's my most prized possession?
My only listener in this room full of fire.
With anything else, I don't have the slightest obsession,
but for this, it can't get any higher.

Does she not have her most prized possession?
I have a forest full of diamond mines.
Ruining this would lead me to depression,
so don't send me bad signs.

This is my most prized possession.
It's far more special than anything expensive.
Keeping this safe and well is my mission.
Next time, I won't be indecisive.

Blinding is the sunlight

Blinding is the sunlight.
Things never felt so right.

Everything seems to be glowing in the sunlight.
From my sneakers to my backpack, it all looks bright.

4:30 P.M., the time most things shine by the sunlight.
7:50 P.M., the time most things are unable to avoid my insight.

That's when I think about the sunlight.
That's when I write with delight.

Repeats in life can feel boring, especially when thinking of sunlights.
Not another day goes by without sunlight and moon-light.

But,
blinding is the sunlight.
Things never felt so right.

Protagonists

You're nice and you're kind,
but you don't remember the feeling of being left out.
Now your place has changed, so you don't mind.
Protagonists don't know what this is about.

"Protect the protagonist" is what they chant.
You don't know the half of it when you're on the throne.
"Get the hell out", that's not what I meant,
but that throne is covered in thorns.

Being a protagonist is temporary,
'cause your shares aren't cares.
That forever glory in your head is imaginary.
I hope that won't sound too much like nightmares.

Acting my age

Too many rules to keep.
Trouble, I ain't even in it that deep.

Sometimes, we must control our rage.
I do, and I'm acting my age.

Some days, I curse the rules,
but most days, I keep the rules.

I'm always trying my best to keep them,
and I "AM" keeping them.

You know even after all that, I wouldn't want the rules to change.
I'm content, and I'm acting my age.

Too good to be true

Every blade is pointed toward us.
Glimmering in the light, they're about to strike.
Whatever we were is now dust.
Crumbling down we might, but that's how things are like.

I can feel it out the door.
Stilettos hit us back and forth.
Notorious to the core.
Maybe like some rubble with no worth.

The rubble was once gold.
Disappointment blows like dynamites.
Everything looks so cold.
The room's full of jagged stalagmites.

We should have kept faith like an oath.
I wish it were real swords that they drew,
but they cut us both.
I knew those old days were too good to be true.

Flawless

These few nights have been sleepless.
I ran far 'til I was breathless.

However, you can't say it's hopeless.
You don't call it mindless.

'Cause things turned out flawless.

Some might say I was clueless,
and if so, they're all heartless.

They might call me reckless,
and if so, they're all thoughtless.

'Cause things turned out flawless.

Three-leaf clover

Red eyes from crying last night.
I haven't been resting, but I'll be alright.
All dizzy from sleeping in late.
I need some time, and I'm not asking them to wait.

Something in my mind is telling me:
"You've got good people on your side.
Your feelings aren't yours to hide.
It didn't work, but you tried."

Like rain pouring from the sky,
you'll see the rainbow when it's over.
I shouldn't leave this place with 'goodbye',
'cause my life is a three-leaf clover.

No one is guilty

No one is guilty for the game.
But they need someone to blame,
so they chose me.
Then, what am I supposed to be?

It's easier to shout
and harder to keep it in.
So, all they do is pout.
It's like their heart is made of tin.

They don't care for your feelings.
"If you're hurt, it's all up to you."
No one should be kneeling.
They all deny to face the greater view.

All I hope is to lose like winners,
but we just paint the mood black.
Everything contains sweets and bitters,
but tasting the sweet is what we all lack.

Recess beat

All the vibes are high.
We can’t be still.
We all know why.
No one wants to keep it chill.

Running up the halls
has never felt so fun.
It’s even louder than the malls.
It takes hours ’til we’re done.

Freedom has never felt so sweet.
Screaming at the top of our lungs.
There’s this kind of recess beat.
Having fun could never feel wrong.

Me

You don't know the half of it.
None of them get how this works.
All they want is wit,
but mostly it's just people they sort.

I know it now.
It's not because I'm wrong.
It's not because I'm right.
Don't know if it's just for show.

It's me.
They happen to hate me.
It's no one other than me.
Could it be any different if you were me?

Some unreasonable temper

No, I don't regret my choice.
I'm actually glad I ghosted her voice.
Go, go and mind yourself.
I'm better than you at minding myself.

She has a temper.
Some unreasonable temper.
She's like a cannon,
and everything will light the fuse of the cannon.

If I do anything unacceptable,
it's me who'll get in trouble.
So, what do you care?
I know you are aware.

She has a temper.
Some unreasonable temper.
She's like a crossbow,
and everything will load the crossbow.

Active

It's a fairy tale kinda thing
when the bell rings,
I become all active.
Makes me want to hit the octave.
I can take this class all day long
and not get anything wrong.
Feels like soaring through the clouds,
feels like waving to a big crowd.

It's a fable kinda thing.
Depression, it can never bring.
My mind switches on to 'active'.
I don't wanna act introvertive.
This class is where I can be strong.
Taylor Swift should make this into a song.
I can't resist but to be loud,
but for me, I really am proud.

Betray your friend day

Today is "betray your friend" day.
There's a price you have to pay
for trusting, caring, and liking your friend.
Leaving scars on hearts as if it's some sort of trend.

That leads me to a thought:
"How many kids are getting stabbed in the back?"
Friendship can't be bought.
If so, you lack.

I'm overjoyin'

I feel like flyin'.
Spent my days tryin'.
They told me :"You can't do it,"
but look who's now killin' it.

Feeling the good in
myself being good at somethin'.
It wasn't a contest, I didn't win,
but this feels like everythin'.

I guess I'm overjoyin',
but I don't really care.
I won't go introvertin'
on how rare this is.

I'm feelin' so lit.
I'll never sit.
Tell me to stop? No I can't stop,
'cause I'm on the top.

I can make words rhyme

Deadlines cover my bulletin board.
Everything is blinking red.
I don't even know what I'm headed toward.
It's complicated in my head.

However, I've done things quite well.
Similar days, I've achieved all,
but how could you tell?
I never left a single mark.

So I think I can do good.
This ain't my first time.
So even when I'm not in the mood,
I can make words rhyme.

Dear. Someone very special

She seems a bit down.
That's when the view out my window
doesn't look like town.
It all looks so hollow.
I'm praying every day at night that she would be more happier,
'cause nothing seems right
when her smile doesn't feel happy.
She listens to my feelings all the time
yet, she doesn't want me to worry.
so she puts on a fake smile.
That's when I feel sorry
that I never got to relate to her like she did,
but I'll try my best and I'll never stop
wishing her only happy days,
'cause I can't be happy on days she's not.

Fatal

The unstable expression on my face says:
"Am I there yet?"
I'm running, but darkness never fades,
but I have to keep my due dates.

I'm told I'm walking to the right place,
but what if I'm going backwards?
Don't wanna be the example of a wrong case.
Darn, why are there so many hard words?

Faltering is my faith,
the faith in myself.
Is this even my pace?
My mind is an elf on the shelf.

Think I'll wish for the silver lining.
The world is cruel and brutal.
Countless conditions for just surviving.
So every flaw you have is fatal.

Last phone call

She will never forget their last phone call;
“One day, I just happened to loathe you.”
Her heart must have had a fall,
’cause she couldn’t hear it beat anymore.

The good days must have been lit,
but now she wants to scream:
“Never was I ever a misfit.”
Things didn’t get better, even in her dreams.

Then she tried to be brave.
Secret notes, conversations, but none of them worked.
Now the problem was grave.
On days she was tricked, they all just smirked.

The day she was found unconscious on the rooftop,
she was happy she discovered what they meant.
So she knew that she could now stop
trying to fill her heart from the dent.

Write verses

You act as if I don't know.
It's actually better for me to not know,
but once you start whispering,
I can feel what you're saying.

In your words, it's being 'nice',
but your talks will spread like mice.
So I'll call you 'mean'.
No one will understand you just because you're in your teens.

How stupid do you think I am?
'Cause I don't give a damn
on any of your curses.
Bet you can't write verses.

Not a single soul

Not a single soul in my school
thinks my drawings are cool.

However, I think they're pretty neat,
pink patterns on a white sheet.

Complaints about my art, I won't hear.
That's what I promised myself last year.

I can make myself better even
when I'm not in the mood.
Really, I'm fine and all good.

Not a single soul can relate.
They have no reason to rate.

Why wouldn't I?

I can feel it.
I can feel all your troubles.
I can't heal it.
I can't make a palace out of rubble.

If I could make things better,
I would.
If I could make you happier,
I would.

Why wouldn't I?

Do you know that
the Christmas lights don't look bright?
Nothing seems right,
when you're down.

[HIDDEN STORIES]

Morning snow ——

'Morning snow' is about the beautiful snowfall of last year. I remember opening the window to touch it as it fell. This year, as the weather was nearing winter, I wondered if snow would fall the way it had last year. I really hope it does.

I wave to you ——

'I wave to you' is about the feeling when a friend who had been nice to you starts acting cold all of a sudden. The most troubling part is that you don't know why.

The kingdom ——

'The kingdom' is about the ordinary life of being in school. A small storybook society is a metaphor to school.

My arsenal ——

'My arsenal' is about facing the people who criticize you. I'm not saying it's about having an argument with them. It's not about being afraid of people who disapprove of you. They group together to look strong on the outside, but they're as weak as twigs on the inside.

Neck high ——

'Neck high' is about a complicated combination of sadness and regret.

Its main thought is "Would the situation not be this bad if I hadn't made this choice?" On days like those, the water does feel like it's up to my neck.

Best protégé ——

'Best protégé' is about losing the weight of always having to fulfill someone's expectations. Living your days just to be yourself feels so free.

Shiny, bright 'n pretty ——

'Shiny, bright 'n pretty' is about the feeling of being left out and your likings being different from the others. In this poetry, I keep saying it's okay, but when you actually read it, you'll get a feeling that I'm saying it's not okay. There were times in my life when I wanted to fit in no matter what, and I guess this poem is about that. But as this poetry says, my aesthetics aren't for the world. I've realized that you don't need to waste your time on trying to be like others.

Dodge the bullet ——

'Dodge the bullet' is about blaming a person in groups. As the poetry says, they shoot the bullet to fill an empty hole.

Frantic ——

'Frantic' is about desperately wanting to remember the moments in your life you wish to go back to. You want to go back in the past but you can't, so you at least want to treasure your memories from your past, but at the same time, you're afraid of forgetting about it.

Your aviation ——

'Your aviation' is dedicated to my brother. I see him studying so much more than I do every day, and he looks really tired. I wanted to let him know that he's not doing this alone and that there are people rooting for him.

Most prized possession ——

'Most prized possession' is about treasuring your favorite thing and not wanting anyone to mess with it.

Blinding is the sunlight ——

'Blinding is the sunlight' is about the glow of sunlight. I remember being inspired for this poem on my way home from school. It was 4:30 P.M. and the sunlight was brightening everything. I wrote this poem at 7:50 P.M. that day.

Protagonists ——

'Protagonists' is about the most popular people among groups. When you're an unpopular person, you feel left out. But somehow when you become a popular person, you can't care for unpopular people even when you know how they feel. The reason is simple: it's because you're getting all the glory right now. You don't want to consider yourself as one of those lonely people but you soon realize the throne you are on is temporary. So I guess this poetry is about that brutal circulation.

Acting my age ——

'Acting my age' is about obeying the rules we have to keep in public places. Obeying the rules is very important, but it's sometimes hard to keep every little detail there is. But of course, rules are rules.

Too good to be true ——

'Too good to be true' is about the feeling when you sense that you have lost someone's faith. When that happens, everything looks dark and aggressive.

Flawless ——

I wrote 'Flawless' after reading a book that had about 550 pages, and I had to read the whole thing in one week. For that week, all I really did was do a little math and read. Some people might think 'reading for a whole week' could be bad since I have more important studying to do. But I think it was worth it.

Three-leaf clover ——

'Three leave clover' is about recovering from self-loathing and looking on the bright side. This poetry carries hope, telling myself I'll be alright.

No one is guilty ——

'No one is guilty' is about the blame you get when your team loses in something. I think everybody has this kind of experience where you get the blame when you were just doing your best. Sometimes the reason for the blame is invalid, and that makes you feel bad. I think we should all face the greater view even when we lose.

Recess beat ——

'Recess beat' is about the excitement and joy of recess. It's like a treat you get for taking classes, don't you think?

Me ——

'Me' is about the feeling of people hating you just for being yourself. There are and there were some times I felt that way.

Some unreasonable temper ——

'Some unreasonable temper' is about the anger of a person who bosses you around. You know what you're doing and you know the consequences, but it can get annoying when someone who's not your parent or teacher minds your business way too much.

Active ——

'Active' is about taking classes about stuffs I'm good at. It's just so much fun. My mind really does switches into 'active'.

Betray your friend day ——

'Betray your friend day' is about November 11th, Pepero Day. You give out peperos to your friends that day. That's why it's the perfect day to betray someone. It's not that complicated, actually. The kid who didn't receive a pepero from someone considered a 'friend' is the one who got betrayed. Simple, isn't it?

I'm overjoyin' ——

'I'm overjoyin' is about the confidence you feel about some-thing you are good at. It really feels like flying.

I can make words rhyme ——

'I can make words rhyme' is about freaking out because there are so many things you need to do before deadlines. But it turns out I've kept every single deadline there was on my bulletin board, and thanks to that, I feel more confident. However there are times when I get all down because I feel like the deadlines are suffocating me, but I manage to brush that kind of feeling off by doing what I really love: writing poetry.

Dear. Someone very special ——

'Dear. Someone very special' is dedicated to my mom. On days I'm not okay, she's always there for me. However, on days my mom is not okay, she sometimes pretends every-thing's fine because she doesn't want me to worry, but I see through her.

Fatal ——

'Fatal' is about the unstableness you feel when trying to fix your flaws and it feels like it's not working. The reason you feel unstable is because that flaw you have is actually 'fatal' when taking tests that deals with your future.

Last phone call ——

'Last phone call' is about the story of a character I read in a book. She had been bullied in school just because her friends decided they didn't like her anymore. She tried so hard to make things right, but her effort didn't do anything to help the situation.

Write verses ——

'Write verses' is about 'whispering'. Whispering is a cruel way to kill someone on the inside. The act of just whispering and shooting glimpse to a person can tell you a million things.

Not a single soul ——

'Not a single soul' is about your drawings being rated by others. But it doesn't really matter since you're content with what you drew. There was actually a time in my life where I cared too much about what others said about my creations. However, I realized that I shouldn't let it have any impact on me.

Why wouldn't I? ——

'Why wouldn't I?' is dedicated to my dad. Sometimes, he has a lot of things on his mind. I wish I could do anything to help him.

Acknowledgement

I'd like to give thanks to...
My family, my teachers and my friends.
They were the best supporters I could ever ask for.

Reflector

An Introductory Course in Communicative English

Published by the Daewangsa Publishing, INC.
176-25 Soraji-ro, Paju-si, Gyeonggi-do, Seoul, Korea, 10863
TEL: 031-947-5471
FAX: 031-947-5470
E-mail: dws74@hanmail.net
Homepage: www.daewangsa.net

ISBN: 978-89-456-9330-3 03840

Price: ₩9,000